# ☼ Collins Care for your

RSPCA
PET GUIDE

# Kitten

# Contents

D0248717

New 3rd Edition
First published in 2004 by
Collins, an imprint of
HarperCollins*Publishers*
77-85 Fulham Palace Road
Hammersmith
London W6 8JB

The Collins website is www.collins.co.uk

Collins is a registered trademark of HarperCollins Publishers Limited

09 08 07 06 05 04
10 9 8 7 6 5 4 3 2 1

First published as *Care for your Kitten* in 1986 by
William Collins Sons & Co Ltd, London
Reprinted once

Second edition published in 1990

Reprinted by
HarperCollins*Publishers*
and subsequently reprinted 12 times

The RSPCA is a registered charity (no. 219099)
The RSPCA website is www.rspca.org.uk

Designed by: SP Creative Design
Editor: Heather Thomas
Design: Rolando Ugolini

A catalogue record for this book is available from the British Library

ISBN 0 00 718271 6

Colour reproduction by Saxon Photolitho, Norfolk
Printed and bound by Printing Express Ltd, Hong Kong

# Foreword

Owning a kitten is great fun but a huge responsibility. All animals need a regular routine and lots of love and attention. But most importantly, pets need owners who are going to stay interested in them and committed to them all their lives.

Anyone who has ever enjoyed the company of a pet knows just how strong the bond can be. Children learn the meaning of loyalty, unselfishness and friendship by growing up with animals. Elderly or lonely people often depend on a pet for company and it has been proved that animals can help in the prevention of and recovery from physical or mental illness.

The decision to bring a pet into your home should always be discussed and agreed by everyone in the family. Bear in mind that parents are ultimately responsible for the health and well-being of the animal for the whole of its lifetime. If you are not prepared for the inevitable expense, time, patience and occasional frustration involved, then the RSPCA would much rather that you didn't have a pet.

Being responsible for a pet will completely change your life but if you make the decision to go ahead, think about offering a home to one of the thousands of animals in RSPCA animal centres throughout England and Wales. There are no animals more deserving of loving owners.

As for the care of your pet, this book should provide you with all the information you need to know to keep it happy and healthy for many years to come. Enjoy the experience!

Steve Cheetham MA, VetMB, MRCVS
Chief Veterinary Offcier RSPCA

# Introduction

Kittens are among the most charming of all young animals. Cuddly, playful and enchanting to watch – few people can resist them. However, it is important to remember that kittens need house training, can be very destructive to carpets and furniture and, where there are young children or elderly folk in the family, can cause accidents or even get trodden underfoot.

▲ A mongrel kitten.

Although a kitten is a very adaptable animal and generally soon makes a good household pet, it does have certain minimum requirements. So before you get a kitten, it is worthwhile asking yourself a few basic questions in order to make sure that it really is the right pet for you.

- Do you have a garden or safe access to the great outdoors?
- Are you at home for at least part of the day, every day?
- Are you willing to put up with the possible damage that claws can do to furnishings?
- Are you willing to bear the cost of vaccinations and any possible veterinary attention? The RSPCA strongly recommends that you take out insurance to cover some of these veterinary costs. (All but those cats kept specifically for breeding should be neutered before six months of age, and all kittens and young cats should be vaccinated against Feline Infectious Enteritis, Feline Influenza and Feline Leukaemia, which require booster vaccinations throughout their lifetime.)
- Are you willing to pay for boarding your cat when you go away on holiday, or have you some caring neighbours who would feed and look after it for you? Please remember however, that on health grounds boarding a kitten is not recommended until the animal is at least four months old.

▼ Young kittens love exploring and are very agile, often climbing up the branches of trees.

The answer to all of these questions should be a resounding 'yes'. If you cannot answer 'yes' to them all (and honesty is very important here), please think very carefully before you get a kitten.

# Pedigree or mongrel?

Once you are quite sure that a kitten is the right pet for you, the next decision to be made is whether to choose a pedigree or a mongrel. For most people, the mongrel or kitten of mixed breeding is the first choice. Generally speaking, these cost little or nothing to buy (many people are only too willing to give a kitten to a good home), but do not forget, of course, that as they grow up they will cost just as much to feed as any pedigree cat. And, naturally, they will need the same amount of love, care and medical attention. Mongrel kittens are generally hardy, with a strong constitution and come in a wide variety of colours and types. The choice is yours.

If you want to know what your animal will look like as it grows up, a pedigree kitten might be the right answer for you. Some breeds have well-known characteristics, like the Siamese with its distinctive voice, or the Longhairs with their dense coats, which require meticulous grooming. Pedigree kittens are, of course, expensive to buy.

However, whether you decide on a pedigree or a mongrel kitten, it is sensible not to take home one that is younger than eight weeks as kittens need to stay with their mother until this time. It is always wise to take your new kitten to your veterinary surgeon for a health check-up within 48 hours of getting it.

◀ Kittens are very active, agile and inquisitive.

# Which sex to choose?

When deciding which sex to choose, it is worth remembering that male kittens will mature at about the age of six months and from then on, unless castrated, will show a tendency to fight, wander and spray an unattractive scent around the place. Female kittens mature at about the same age, and will then come into season from spring onwards, once every two to three months for about eight months of the year. So unless you turn your home into a high-security prison, they will almost certainly become pregnant and produce many litters.

On the whole, therefore, unless you plan to buy a pedigree cat and breed from it, it is more sensible to have your kitten neutered, whether it is a male or a female. Neutering is a straightforward operation for your veterinary surgeon to perform. It is not cruel and nor is it unfair to the cat. For the vast majority of people who want to own a kitten primarily as a pet, it is the only practical and responsible thing to do (see opposite). It is, of course, simpler and therefore less expensive to neuter a tom cat than to neuter a female. If you do intend to neuter your kitten, you will find that the differences in character between a male and a female are minimal after the operation has been carried out. Once neutered, there is often more variety between individual animals than there is between the sexes. Whether you decide on getting a male or female kitten, this is a matter of personal choice.

## How to tell a male from a female

Sexing a kitten is a relatively easy procedure. Lift the kitten on to a table and then raise its tail. If you look closely, you will see that the distance between the anus and the urinary tract opening is very short in a female, and rather longer in a male. Moreover, the opening tends to be slit-shaped in females and rounded in males.

# Neutering

The RSPCA strongly recommends that any cat that is to be kept as a household pet should be neutered. In the Society's view, it is in the best interests of both the cat and its owner. The exception is if you have a pedigree kitten which you intend to show and later use for stud purposes.

Some people take the view that it is 'unnatural' to neuter a kitten and they believe that it will adversely affect its character or its weight. There are other people, meanwhile, who feel that it is wrong to deny the animal its basic instincts. It can be safely said, however, that neutering will not make your kitten overweight when it grows older, unless it is regularly overfed, and nor will it have a detrimental effect on its character. As for basic instincts: too frequent matings can result in a tired and overworn female and a tom that is battlescarred and sometimes badly wounded from fights over queens.

▲ An un-neutered female cat can have as many as three pregnancies a year, with five or six kittens in each litter.

It is worth remembering that a female will come into season about every two or three weeks for around eight months of the year. As time goes on, it will become increasingly difficult to prevent her from becoming pregnant and just as difficult to find a first-class home for every kitten. Many thousands of unwanted cats and kittens are destroyed each year, so it is obviously wiser to spay your female.

## The best time to neuter

Male kittens can be castrated before they are six months old. This will stop them spraying unpleasant tom cat scent everywhere, wandering off after females and disappearing for days at a time. It will also prevent them from fighting and being afflicted with the attendant injuries – which might well need veterinary attention.

Female kittens can be spayed from about the age of three months onwards. Spaying usually costs more than castrating a male, but it is also a routine operation for your veterinary surgeon to perform and has no harmful effects on the kitten.

# Breed varieties

▲ Blue Point Birman

▲ Golden Persian

▶ Although longhaired cats will need regular grooming, kittens like this Black Persian can prove irresistible.

Pedigree cats are usually divided into the following groups: Persian or Longhair, Semi-Longhair, Shorthair, Foreign Shorthair and Oriental.

## Persian or Longhair

Today's longhaired pedigree cats are thought to have originated in Turkey and they were first seen in Europe in the sixteenth century. They were called Angora cats, after the old Turkish city of that name (now called Ankara). Other long-coated cats were brought from Persia and from the descendants of these two types we now have a wide range of Persian or Longhair varieties from which to choose. Persian cats have round, broad heads; short, wide noses; large, round eyes; and tiny, tufted ears. Their bodies are chunky and set on thick, short legs with large, round paws. The varieties are named after their coat colour, so Persians may be Black, White, Blue, Chocolate, Lilac, Red or Cream, and also Tabby, Tortoiseshell and a range of bicolours, including Blue and White and Red and White. In addition, varieties have been bred with 'tipped' guard hairs that are a different colour from the undercoat, giving rise to a range of beautiful effects, such as Chinchilla Golden, Shaded Cameo and Black Smoke. Persian cats with 'Siamese' colouring are called Colourpoints and are available in the whole spectrum of point colours.

## Semi-Longhairs

Other longhaired breeds and varieties of cat exist but they are less extreme in their features than the Persians, have longer, slightly finer bodies and, often, rather less luxurious fur.

The Birman has 'Siamese' colouring, but it also has pure white paws and lower legs. The Ragdoll also has 'Siamese' patterning, and various white markings are called for in show specimens. Maine Coon cats came from the United States and are an old breed – longhaired and with a very wide range of permitted colours and patterns.

The Turkish Angora is also found in a large range of colours, while the Turkish Van, often called the swimming cat, is white with patches of auburn or cream on the face and the tail.

Balinese cats are long-coated versions of Siamese, and should have the same characteristics, whereas the Somali is a long-coated variety of the well-known Abyssinian cat.

## Shorthairs

The British Shorthair is similar in bodily conformation to the Persian, but it has a very short, dense coat. The colour range is extremely similar to that of the Persian, with the addition of a range of beautiful spotted varieties.

The Exotic Shorthair is a short-coated version of the Persian and is, in fact, bred from Persian and British Shorthair parentage in a large range of colour varieties. The interesting tailless Manx cat, which originated in the Isle of Man, is a short-haired variety which is found in a wide range of colours. There is also a

▲ British Shorthair

▼ Manx cat

▲ Exotic Shorthair

longhaired variety of Manx cat, which is called the Cymric. The Scottish Fold is similar to the British Shorthair in its size, shape and colour, but it is distinguished by its forward-folded ears, which give it the appearance of wearing a bonnet.

## Foreign Shorthairs

This group covers a wide variety of quite different breeds, though they all tend to be slim and lithe, with longer faces than the

▲ Cornish Rex

British Shorthairs, and with large ears and long, fine tails. Abyssinians have a uniquely ticked coat and are thought to resemble the cats of Ancient Egypt. The Russian Blue is a beautiful slate grey in colour, with a short, dense coat, upright ears and green eyes, while another breed of the same coat colour, the Korat, has a different coat texture, and a heart-shaped face. Burmese cats come in a whole range of coat colours and are renowned for their very short, glossy coats. The eye colour in the Burmese should be yellow or gold. Burmilla cats, bred from Burmese and Chinchilla Persians, have

▲ Abyssinian

beautifully tipped coats which seem to sparkle, while the Bombay, bred from Burmese and Shorthaired Blacks, looks like patent leather.

Rex cats are curly-coated. There are two main breeds, named after the English counties in which they were first discovered. The Cornish Rex, very long, lithe and Oriental in appearance, usually sports a luxuriantly curled coat, while the Devon Rex has a different body structure, and a soft, wavy coat.

▶ Burmese

## Orientals

The term 'Oriental' in cats covers the Siamese and those short-coated varieties that are derived from the Siamese. All these cats should be slim and lithe; with wedge-shaped heads; large pointed ears; long, slim legs; and long, pointed tails.

They are intelligent, inquisitive animals. Siamese have their coat colour restricted to the 'points': the face, or mask, the ears, legs and paws, and the tail. All Siamese cats have blue eyes. The original Royal Cats of Siam were pale fawn with very dark brown/black points, and they were called Sealpoint.

There are now many colour varieties, some of which occurred naturally, and some of which were produced by selective breeding. Siamese-derived Orientals have lost the gene that restricts the colour to the points, and, along with that gene, the one that is responsible for the blue eye colour. Orientals are found in the same colour range as the Siamese, but generally have brilliant green eyes. The Oriental or Foreign White, however, is pure white and has deep blue eyes.

▲ Siamese adult

◀ Sealpoint Siamese kittens

# Biology

**Tail** The tail has many uses. It acts as a balancing mechanism when the kitten is climbing and jumping; it provides warmth when it is sleeping; and, very importantly, it is also a signalling device. The tail upright and waving cheerfully is often the way a kitten will greet its owner. But the tail fluffed out and twice its normal size is a means of indicating both alarm and warning. When a small kitten's tail becomes giant-sized in the presence of a strange dog, the dog should probably watch out.

**Movement** A kitten's skeleton is specially developed to provide extraordinary flexibility. This is achieved by means of an ultramobile backbone which enables the kitten to enter all kinds of postures. For example, a kitten can arch its back into an upside-down 'U'; bend itself in half; sleep in a circle; and rotate the front half of its spine while the back half remains stable. By the time a kitten reaches physical maturity, at around seven or eight months, it is generally able to jump up to five times its own height.

**Claws** A kitten's claws are a crucial part of its defence system. They are also a weapon of attack and an all important aid to climbing. Made of keratin, the horny protein that forms the outer layer of the epidermis, the claws are part of the skin, not the skeleton. A kitten's claws should not usually need to be trimmed; normal healthy usage will keep them the proper length. Only the front paws have a dew claw.

**Ears** A kitten has super-sensitive hearing, although white kittens (especially those with blue eyes) do have a tendency towards congenital deafness. Most of the kitten's ear is hidden within the skull bones. The pinna, or ear flap, simply funnels sound waves down to the ear drum, which passes them to the inner ear. A kitten's ears are also a valuable means of expressing anger, fear and pleasure. For instance, the ears of an angry kitten are usually upright and furled back, whereas a happy and interested kitten has pricked up, perky ears. Later on, the ears play an important part in the animal's social life, especially when courting.

**Eyes** All kittens are born with their eyes closed – their eyes begin to open when they are between five and ten days old, depending on the breed. To begin with, all kittens have blue eyes; their adult eye colour will not start to emerge until around 12 weeks. Cats have a wide variety of eye colour, ranging through orange, copper, yellow, hazel, green and blue (as in some white cats and in the Siamese). A kitten does not see as well as an adult cat until it is around three months old, but from then on vision becomes perhaps the most important of the cat's senses.

**Whiskers** Kittens are generally born with a full set of whiskers. They usually have about a dozen whiskers on each upper lip plus a few on each cheek, as well as tufts over the eyes and bristles on the chin. Whiskers grow from hair follicles which are well supplied with nerve-endings so they are very sensitive to touch. Because the extent of a cat's whiskers, from one tip to the other, is the same as the maximum width of its body, they probably provide the means whereby a kitten or cat can judge the width of an opening.

**Teeth** Kittens are born with 'baby' teeth. These start to be shed around the age of 12 weeks, and their full set of 30 teeth have generally grown in by about seven months. By this age the kitten will have become a young cat and will have a set of twelve incisors, four canines, ten premolars and four molars. A cat's teeth should be checked regularly for build-up of tartar and, if this has developed, the cat should be taken to the veterinary surgeon for them to be scaled.

**Tongue** The tongue is an essential aid to effective grooming. A kitten's tongue is long, muscular and very mobile, and its middle is covered with small projections, or papillae, which give it the characteristic 'emery board' feel. The tongue is also vital for lapping milk or water, which the kitten should be able to do from about four weeks of age. When lapping, the tongue becomes spoon-shaped, and the kitten swallows after about every four or five laps.

# Picking out a healthy kitten

Whether you choose a pedigree or mongrel, male or female, you will still want a strong, healthy kitten. If you follow these simple guidelines you should be able to pick out a healthy youngster. So, look for:

● **A nicely rounded animal** The kittens should feel plump and must be at least eight weeks old before they leave their mother. Avoid any skinny kittens or those with distended tummies. Such kittens are likely to be infested with intestinal worms.

● **Bright, clear eyes**
Do not be tempted to take kittens with runny eyes or sneezing noses, or which have a noticeable 'third eyelid' (see page 33).

● **Dry, clean tail**
Reject any kitten which has a sore anus, wet tail, or diarrhoea, which is indicated by yellow stains on the rear fur.

● **A healthy coat** Do a quick check for fleas – many kittens have them and their presence is indicated by small black grits in the fur at the base of the ears, and on the spine towards the tail, as well as on the tummy. These can be dealt with quite easily (see page 40).

● **Clean ears** If a kitten has signs of dry, dark grey deposits in its ears, it is probably affected by ear mites. Your veterinary surgeon can easily deal with this problem, but you ought to be aware of their existence.

## Longhair or Shorthair?

Remember that a fluffy kitten will almost certainly grow up to be a longhaired cat, and longhaired cats need a regular daily brush and comb if they are not to suffer from matted coats and dangerous hair balls (see page 23). If you have not got time to spend grooming a longhaired cat, do not get a fluffy kitten, no matter how appealing it may be. It is much better to go for shorthaired varieties, as their coats are a great deal easier to look after. Some shorthaired kittens do have a slightly fluffy appearance to begin with, which can be misleading. However, if the mother is shorthaired and the father is thought to be, you can be fairly certain your kitten will grow up to be a shorthaired cat.

## Where to get your kitten

The best place to obtain a pet kitten is from friends, or by answering advertisements in the local paper. It is a good idea to see the litter with the mother cat when you make your choice, so you can ascertain that the complete family is healthy and well-cared for. Kittens are often available in pet shops, but those for sale may have come from more than one source and they could have an infection. Such kittens might also have been taken away from their mother before having been completely weaned, which causes digestive problems.

▼ Pewter, Smoke and Shaded Silver Persian kittens: the choice can be bewildering if you decide upon a particular breed. Books, local clubs and breed societies will all offer advice on how to avoid pitfalls.

# Housing

## Comfortable sleeping quarters

Kittens spend a great deal of time asleep and they do need plenty of rest, so a warm, dry, comfortable bed is essential. Cardboard boxes, especially deep-sided ones (to keep out draughts), make useful beds. They can be lined with newspaper, which is warm, inexpensive and easily changed. It is also possible to buy wicker cat beds, or ones that are made from durable plastic which are easily cleaned.

That said, it is more than likely that your kitten will choose some other place for its afternoon nap, and give no more than a passing sniff to the bed you have prepared for it. Do not worry if this happens; this is just an example of a kitten's independent nature. However, if there is a place where you really do not want your kitten to sleep (on your bed, or on a baby's, for example), then you must firmly shut the door and make that room inaccessible to the kitten.

## Litter trays

House training is the first lesson every kitten needs to learn. Fortunately, most of them are instinctively clean. You will need to provide your kitten with a leak-proof tray or box (plastic or enamel is best), which should be about 40 x 25 cm (16 x 10 in), and put it in some convenient corner. The tray can be filled with sand, dry earth or the sort of cat litter you can buy from any pet shop or most large supermarkets. The sides of the tray need to be high enough to stop litter being scattered about by over-zealous kittens. In fact, some people find a large washing-up bowl makes a good litter tray, as it has deep sides and can be easily scrubbed out. Hooded litter trays are available; these provide ideal facilities for kittens that like their toilet arrangements to be private.

▼ A kitten using a litter tray in the house.

### Cleaning

Hot water and soap are all you need. Bleach can be used from time to time, provided it is thoroughly rinsed away, but avoid household detergents, many of which contain coal tar and carbolic derivatives which can be dangerous to kittens. It is a good idea not to empty the tray completely each time you clean it but to add a little of the old litter to the fresh, at least until the kitten is completely house trained. A litter tray must be kept clean and must be emptied regularly, otherwise the fastidious kitten will simply refuse to use it. If you should be unlucky enough to find a few accidents on your carpet, then a spray of plain soda water can help to remove the smell, and there are several effective proprietary brands of stain removers and other removers available.

## Going outside

If you have a garden to which your kitten has access, you will probably find that in time the kitten will tend to go outside, in preference to the litter tray (in warm weather, at least). If there are areas in the garden that are forbidden to the kitten — new seed beds, for instance — these are best made inaccessible by the use of chicken wire or some other form of netting.

▲ A cat flap provides a kitten with freedom and independence.

## Cat flaps

Until your kitten has reached the stage where it really knows its way around the house and the garden, it is best not to let it out without some kind of supervision. When it is confident of its home and surroundings, and it has been fully immunized, a cat flap fitted to an outside door will provide the freedom and independence that cats enjoy. It is important to fit the cat flap correctly and at the right height, and to teach your kitten to use it correctly. The spring should be strong enough to close the flap, but not so strong as to trap the young cat's head or tail as it passes through. There are several types available which can be bolted or set to open in only one direction. If necessary, older cats may wear a radio-controlled device on a collar which opens a specifically designed cat flap, and prevents entry by stray cats. The majority of cat injuries occur at night, so although your kitten is probably liveliest at night and might want to stay out, it is wiser and safer to make sure it's inside. Town cats or kittens, especially, should be kept indoors after dark and given a litter tray.

## House cats

It is possible to keep a kitten or cat without allowing it to go outside, but a number of difficulties can arise and, unless there are exceptional circumstances, the RSPCA does not recommend keeping it in this way. Restricted living conditions often lead to boredom, which, in turn, encourages destructive habits like carpet-ripping and furniture-scratching.

# Introducing the new kitten

## Travelling comfortably

Before you bring home a new kitten, it is sensible to carry out some advance preparations which will make life more comfortable both for the kitten and the family. First of all, you will need some kind of travelling basket in which to transport the kitten. These range in quality from the cheapest cardboard carrier to the more expensive wicker, wire or plastic variety. Whichever you choose, it should measure at least 50 x 28 x 28 cm (20 x 11 x 11 in). A travelling basket is a good investment for every cat owner, since it will be essential for taking your kitten to the veterinary surgery (for vital vaccinations) as well as all the other occasions when you may need to transport it. Many cats are upset by the confinement and the noise and smell of a car or a bus. You should accustom your kitten to associating its travelling basket with treats to lessen the ordeal (see page 27).

## Settling in safely

Once your kitten is safely home, it is best to confine it, for the first few days, to just one room in the house. The room chosen should be free from hazards, such as open chimneys and trailing electrical cables (see pages 36–7). Kittens can and do find their way into the tiniest of spaces and can be very difficult to extricate. There should be no open windows or doors when the kitten first arrives, for even the most placid

▶ A plastic-coated wire mesh door will afford a cat a good view of its surroundings, something many appreciate. When you bring your kitten home, open the door of the pet carrier and give the kitten time to come out and explore its new surroundings.

of kittens may be upset by its first journey into strange surroundings. Make sure that the kitten knows where its litter tray is, and put its bed in a warm, draught-free place. You could pop a small alarm clock with a loud tick into its bedding. The rhythm of the ticking will remind the kitten of its mother's heart-beat, and may help it to settle down more quickly.

## Handling the kitten

Remember that kittens need lots of rest and sleep; if there are small children in the family, be sure to explain this to them. A young kitten, which has just been removed from its mother and brothers and sisters, will not unnaturally be a little homesick at first, so plenty of care, affection and understanding is called for. Some kittens, too, are more timid than others, and will need longer to adjust to their new surroundings. If this appears to be the case, do not rush your kitten, but allow it to 'hide away' if it feels like it. It will emerge as soon as it feels more confident. During the first few days, do not allow the kitten to be over-handled by strangers or squeezed too affectionately by youngsters.

▲ Make sure that the first meeting between a new kitten and other more established pets in the household is supervised.

# First meeting with other pets

If you already have a dog or another cat in the household, it is very important that the first meeting between the newcomer and the resident pet is under strict supervision. It is often sensible to keep the older pet shut up for a while, to allow the newcomer to get used to its scent. Cats and kittens being introduced to one another react primarily to scent, and it is sometimes helpful to rub a little talcum powder into the coats of each animal, under the chin and around the base of the tail. Most

▼ Dogs and young kittens frequently become great friends, provided first introductions are tactfully made.

mature animals are tolerant of young ones, but occasionally jealousy can turn to aggression so make sure that introductions take place slowly, with 'retreating' space available for all concerned. Or get a mesh play pen to protect the kitten while the established pet learns to accept its presence. Do not let resident pets feel neglected as this may worsen their natural jealousy and lead to behavioural reactions, such as aggression and persistent attention-seeking.

# Feeding

A sensible feeding programme, which means offering the right food in the right proportions, is essential to a kitten's healthy growth and well-being. Feeding regimes vary, but, basically, you can use either prepared tinned food or dried food to feed your kitten.

## Using prepared food

Most prepared foods contain all the necessary vitamins and minerals to provide a balanced diet for your kitten. Some contain more moisture than others, and some have a greater concentration of meat. When using these foods, it is extremely important to read and follow the manufacturer's instructions, and feed the kitten accordingly. With dried food, always ensure that there is an adequate water supply.

## Feeding suggestions

▼ Meat meals should always be fed fresh and should never be allowed to go stale.

Concentrated diets that are specially designed for kittens should be fed from weaning. Multiple small feeds should be fed throughout the day, divided into at least four to five meals per day. The manufacturers' instructions should be followed for different foods. At six months, the

growth diet may be changed to an adult formulation. The frequency of feeding may be reduced to twice daily but multiple feeds can continue throughout the day. This fits in with the cat's natural preference to snack feed during the day and night.

## Feeding guidelines

- **Never** feed your kitten meals straight from the refrigerator; its food should always be at room temperature.
- **Never** leave food down. If a meal is not cleared in 20 minutes or so, then remove it. Feed less next time.
- **Never** feed your kitten on soiled plates. Always wash its dishes in hot water with detergent, then rinse well and allow to drain dry. Have a set of dishes just for your kitten's use.
- **Never** feed your kitten with fish or poultry bones or skin.
- **Never** try to wean your kitten off meat, even if you are a vegetarian yourself. Cats cannot get all the protein they need from non-meat sources.

▲ Fresh water should be available at all times.

## How much food?

Some kittens are much greedier than others and some grow more quickly, so there are many variations in feeding programmes. However, the basic ground rule is 'feed to appetite'. If your kitten is constantly leaving its food, you are possibly giving it too much; if, on the other hand, it is always shouting for more to eat, consider whether or not you should increase its intake (but first look carefully at its condition and do not be taken in by mere greed). Kittens tend not to overeat and should reach their adult bodyweight by six months.

## Feeding orphaned kittens

The hand rearing of kittens may be necessary if the mother has an inadequate supply of milk, is sick or the litter is orphaned. Orphaned kittens have two main requirements: a suitable environment and nutrition.
- Their pen should be insulated and heated with either a heat pad or a hot water bottle – care must be taken that the kittens do not get burnt or over-heat.
- After feeding the mother would normally lick around the anogenital area to stimulate the kitten to pass urine and faeces. This can be simulated by using a damp piece of cotton wool or kitchen towel.

▶ Orphaned kittens can be fed with a substitute cat's milk via a small syringe or feeding bottle.

• Between 16–21 days, kittens no longer require stimulation to urinate and defecate; from 28 days they are able to control body temperature.
• Kittens need cats' milk, and a substitute milk is now commercially available – cows' or goats' milk is an inadequate substitute. The milk can be administered slowly by using a small syringe or feeding bottle, following the manufacturers' feeding guidelines.
• When the kittens begin to explore their surroundings at around four weeks, a high-quality kitten food can be introduced. This can be mixed with a milk substitute to begin with and then fed separately.

## Milk and water

All kittens need constant access to a fresh supply of drinking water. If a kitten does not appear to be drinking enough, it may be because it does not like the water (nowadays some of the chemicals in tap water are most unpalatable to cats). If this appears to be the case, then try offering clean rainwater or filtered or bottled water.

Milk is not essential for kittens, and, indeed, some do not like it one bit. It can often cause diarrhoea, so only feed it sparingly, if at all. Remember that milk is, strictly speaking, a food, not a drink. However, if you want to feed your kitten milk, then you should use a cats' milk substitute which is available from supermarkets.

# Grooming

## Benefits of grooming

If you were simply unable to resist getting a fluffy-coated kitten, then you must be prepared for regular daily grooming sessions. The sooner these start the better, as kittens are much more amenable to brushing and combing when grooming starts at an early age. However, all kittens and cats will benefit from grooming at certain periods in the year, when their coats begin to moult. This is usually in the spring and, to a lesser extent, in the autumn. It is very important that they should not swallow too many loose hairs when they groom themselves as these matt up in the stomach and form hair balls, which can cause serious illnesses. Grooming also keeps dandruff to a minimum and, of course, gives you a chance to check your kitten's skin condition carefully, thereby ensuring that any lumps or bumps are discovered and attended to promptly.

▲ Short-coated cats will only need a quick groom with a comb or brush.

## Basic equipment

The equipment that you require for grooming your kitten is very simple. All you will need is a soft brush, a wide-toothed comb, a fine-toothed flea comb, and, lastly, a damp chamois or wash leather.

## Shorthaired kittens

Shorthaired kittens will certainly need less attention paid to their coat as they can effectively groom themselves, but keep a close eye on them at moulting time. Brushing with a soft brush will pay dividends, or you can run a damp chamois leather over the coat to pick up any loose hairs quickly. Just hold the leather in both hands and

◀ Glove brushes are good for stripping loose hairs from shorthaired or longhaired cats. There are several types with varying degrees of grip.

draw it over the kitten from its head to its tail. Hand grooming is beneficial to both the kitten and owner and helps bonding between the two. Stroke the kitten fairly firmly from head to tail with clean, dry hands.

A kitten with a dull coat or one that moults excessively may not be in the best of health, perhaps due to a poor diet (see page 21).

## Longhaired kittens

As already mentioned, longhaired kittens need combing daily, otherwise their fur gets into a nasty matted mess, which is not only unsightly but also uncomfortable and potentially a hazard to health. The fur should be combed through thoroughly, but gently, starting at the head and gradually working back towards the base of the tail, using a wide-toothed comb and combing against the lie of the coat to separate each hair. It is important to groom under the body and around the base of the tail where the hair is extra fine. If regular grooming is neglected, then dense tangles will have to be cut out and very bad cases may even need veterinary attention.

▲ Longhairs, such as this Persian, will need regular and intensive grooming to keep their coats silky and free of tangles.

▲ Feel your way through your cat's coat and use your fingers to gently unravel any loose knots and tangles you find.

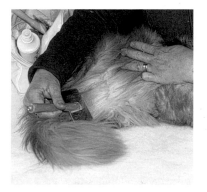

▲ Brush or comb the fur away from the cat's head towards the tail.

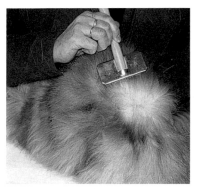

▲ Comb or brush the fur in the opposite direction, without dragging it.

▲ Gently brush the ruff of fur around the cat's neck and head.

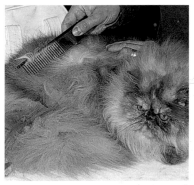

▲ Carefully comb or cut out any knots and tangles that remain.

▲ Brush the fur underneath, teasing out any knots with your fingers or a comb.

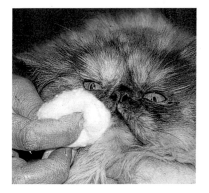

▲ Check the ears, nose and eyes, gently wiping away any mucus.

# Handling and training

Kittens learn all about life at an early age. Known as the socialization period, this lasts until about 12 weeks. The kitten meets potentially frightening objects, such as washing machines and vacuum cleaners, during this period. If it gets used to them by gentle introduction, it will accept them for the rest of its life. The same applies to meeting other animals. Accordingly, owners should make a positive effort to get a kitten out and about as soon as it is safe to do so.

## Handling a kitten or young cat

It is always preferable to pick up a kitten or a young cat by putting one hand underneath its chest and the other around its hind legs, so that the animal's entire weight is supported. If the kitten is then turned towards the handler, it can cling to clothing for extra security.

It is *never* a good idea to pick up a kitten by the scruff of the neck as this puts too much strain on its body and internal organs. (Only mother cats should pick up kittens by the scruff of the neck, and even they only do this when the kitten is very tiny.)

Children will often play with a kitten by picking it up just by its forelegs or even by its tail. Although many cats will put up with much more than ought to be expected, all the members of the family should be taught to treat a kitten very gently.

You should accustom your kitten to being handled all over its head and body, particularly if it is long-coated and must be groomed daily.

▶ How to pick up your kitten the correct way. Always be sure to support the kitten's full weight. Support it under the bottom and hind legs with one hand and use the other hand to support the chest.

Make handling a pleasure for your kitten by being gentle. Soon the kitten should allow you to look inside its ears and mouth without flinching or trying to bite you. You must exercise patience and combine the serious examination with stroking or scratching the top of its head; these areas are sensitive to touch and will give a pleasurable sensation to the kitten.

## Training

Kittens learn quickly and if you want to train your kitten you will need to start early. You will also need lots of patience! Make sure that the training sessions are fun for all concerned. Short and frequent periods of training are better than long ones now and again.

Kittens can be trained to come to your call. Put your kitten across the room from where you are and call its name, using a fairly high, clear voice, followed by the command 'Come'. When it obeys, make a big fuss of it and offer a small titbit as a reward.

Perhaps the most important aspect of training is to teach your kitten to go willingly into its carrying box or basket. You should make this a special event by putting a favourite plaything or titbit into the carrier before shutting the kitten in for a short while, then open the lid and make a great fuss of it. Turning the carrier into part of a game will pay dividends when you need to take your kitten to the veterinary surgery or on a journey.

Some kittens respond to training as 'retrievers' and, with very little encouragement, will chase after and return to you such things as catnip mice, paper balls, and spidery toys made from twisted pipe-cleaners.

As the kitten gets older, you will find that a sharp clap of the hands accompanying the word 'No', when it misbehaves, proves a kind, effective training method.

It's natural for kittens to jump up on high places, scratch furniture and chase birds. If you don't want your kitten to do certain things, you must make that clear from the beginning with a firm 'No'. Remember, however, that although you can train cats not to claw chairs or jump on to the china cabinet, you will not train them to ignore their predatory instincts. Kittens are very sensitive to criticism, so do not be too harsh. Correction should be firm but gentle. Scolding a kitten for any misdemeanour after the event is meaningless – it will simply not understand why you are cross.

▼ Get your kitten used to being handled from an early age. Take time out to stroke and groom it.

# Exercise

Although kittens have a great deal of energy (like most youngsters), they also need plenty of rest. Although your kitten is likely to play furiously for 10 minutes or so, it will then be more than ready to sleep for several hours. It is very important, therefore, that young children should not try to wake the kitten while it is sleeping.

## Outdoor exercise

Once you are quite sure that your kitten really knows its way around the house, it can be safely let outside to play, provided it can always get back quickly to the security of its home and bed. If you have a fitted cat flap, this will mean that your kitten can always beat a safe retreat if the outside world suddenly looks too alarming.

## The pros and cons of collars

You might be considering whether a collar would be advisable for your kitten, with an identity tag showing your name and address. A collar is acceptable provided that the kitten has no overwhelming objection to wearing it, and that it is not more than about 1 cm ($^1/_2$ in) wide and is of the 'snap apart' variety.

The RSPCA also recommends that your kitten is microchipped – ask your vet for further details.

▶ Any opportunity for outdoor exercise is very important for kittens. Try to make time to play with your kitten in the garden.

◀ This may seem a bit extreme but some city cats will enjoy being fitted with a harness and lead and taken for walks.

▼ If your cat wears a collar, take care that it is of the snap apart variety to prevent accidents happening when it is outside in the garden or climbing trees. Although they rarely get stuck, cats sometimes climb too high and need rescuing.

A collar does, of course, provide a useful means of identification, but it also carries an element of risk as it could get caught on a branch, for example, and the kitten might be unable to escape. While a collar is especially useful after moving house, for instance, it might be wisest to remove it when you feel that any danger of your kitten straying is over.

## Indoor exercise

It is a good plan to encourage your kitten to play in the house as well as outside. Provide a selection of suitable toys for it to play with: old cardboard boxes to hide in, cotton reels to chase, and pieces of string

to pounce on are all much appreciated, as are large paper bags which rustle. Some kittens are particularly keen on toy mice stuffed with catnip. Be wary of toys made of plastic, as they can be harmful if chewed.

Kittens are very fond of playing with feathers. A stiff feather about 12 cm (5 in) long will provide hours of fun as the kitten bats it around from paw to paw, tosses it in the air and carries it around, growling. A long feather, such as the tail feather from a peacock, makes an excellent decoy. You can exercise your kitten by getting it to chase the feather tip, moved tantalizingly to and fro across the floor. Don't encourage your kitten to play with man-made yarn, which causes intestinal problems if swallowed.

▲ Kittens love to play so provide plenty of toys and suitable items to keep it amused and prevent boredom setting in.

## Provide a scratching post

If your kitten is not going to spend a lot of time outdoors, or if your garden is short of trees, it might be wise to provide a scratching post. All kittens' claws need sharpening from time to time and this is best not done on your furniture and curtains. A simple log kept in a convenient place, or a small post covered with a piece of cloth (some kittens prefer this), will usually be quite sufficient. If, despite this, your kitten does show a tendency to head for the furniture, you should discourage it gently but firmly, and point it instead towards the scratching post. If you want your kitten to use a scratching post, it is best to encourage it to do so from an early age. Good habits are more easily formed when an animal is young and easily trained.

▶ Kittens will play very happily with a variety of items. Even a rolled-up ball of foil can provide lots of harmless fun.

◀ Some scratching posts are quite elaborate and they can be used outside in the garden as well as inside the house. They also enable kittens to play and to explore their environment safely.

# The healthy kitten

## Vaccinations and health checks

If you do not have a certificate to show that your new kitten has been fully vaccinated, you should make an appointment with your veterinary surgeon, and take your pet along, packed safely in its carrier. Before administering the vaccine, the vet will check the health of your kitten thoroughly and, depending on the make and type of vaccine used, either one dose, or two doses with a 14-day interval between, may be given. Your kitten should not be allowed to come into contact with other cats which may not be vaccinated until its immunity is complete.

The veterinary surgeon will tell you whether or not a course of worming medicine for your kitten is advisable, and may also discuss a suitable date for neutering. He or she will check the kitten's teeth, to see that they are all coming through properly and that there is no sign of gum disorder. If you ask, you will be shown how to examine and clean the ears, and how to extend and clip back the kitten's claws.

It is very important that you establish a happy relationship with your veterinary surgeon while your kitten is in good health. You may need their services some day in an emergency situation.

▼ Healthy kittens will find endless amusement in the simplest things, and love holes and tunnels that they can jump in and out of.

# What to look out for

If your kitten deviates from any of the 'signs of health' that are listed on page 34, seek veterinary advice at once. So many cat illnesses and ailments can be cured if they are caught in the earliest stages.

## Signs of health

If the kitten is eating normally, its faeces and urine are passed regularly and are inoffensive, its eyes are bright, its coat glossy and it is playful and active, then there is likely to be little wrong with its general health.

## Signs of illness

The warning signs of illness include loss of appetite, listlessness and an 'open' appearance of the coat, due to the hairs being held semi-erect in an attempt to reduce a raised body temperature. Cats have three eyelids: the upper lid, the lower lid, and the nictitating membrane, or 'haw', which passes across the eye from the inner corner. When a kitten has a raised temperature, or is incubating an illness, the 'haw' is often visible as a film-like skin across the inner corner of the eye.

Sometimes teething troubles cause the 'haw' to show, and a quick look inside the mouth might confirm this. Kittens' second teeth will often erupt before the milk teeth are shed, and having both sets present makes the mouth crowded and the gums so sore that the kitten may not want to eat. Giving long strips of raw meat might help the kitten to remove the loose milk teeth. Otherwise they may need professional removal.

## Diarrhoea

The most common problem that is encountered in an otherwise healthy kitten is diarrhoea; this is almost always caused by incorrect diet. You may be feeding too much food; it may be too rich, too cold, or just indigestible. If your kitten was obtained from a reliable source, you should have a diet sheet or details of the food on which it was weaned, and you should try to continue with the same feeding regime for a few weeks. Some kittens,

◄ Kittens at play will act out the stalking, pouncing and fighting behaviours of their wild relatives.

especially those with Oriental forebears, are unable to digest whole milk and some dairy products. In any case of diarrhoea, these should be withheld.

Over-zealous use of some cleaning agents on floors, carpets and litter trays can also cause diarrhoea in young kittens so always take great care in using any chemical products, and make sure that the kitten does not pad around on wet floors or on contaminated soil. In the garden, keep it away from chemical fertilizers, soil dressings and slug pellets. Nor should it come into contact with any form of paint or wood preservative. Cats are attracted to the anti-freeze substance used in car engines, which is lethal to them, so keep your kitten out of your garage.

## Signs of health

| | |
|---|---|
| **Abdomen** | Without wounds, growths and sores; not distended or unduly sensitive. |
| **Anus** | It should be clean, with no staining or scouring; motions should be passed without persistent constipation or diarrhoea. |
| **Appetite** | Good; weight maintained with steady growth; no persistent vomiting. |
| **Breathing** | It should be even, quiet, with no wheezing or coughing. |
| **Claws** | There should be no splits, thorns, splinters or damaged pads. |
| **Coat** | Should be clean, well-groomed, glossy; free from parasites, their eggs and droppings, loose hairs and scurviness; no baldness or patches. |
| **Demeanour** | The kitten should be watchful, even at rest; quickly responsive to sounds; playful, lively and contented. |
| **Ears** | These should be pricked to catch sounds; free of discharge; no irritation, scratching or shaking of the head. |
| **Eyes** | Clear, not bloodshot; third eyelid (thin membrane that sometimes flicks across the eyes during illness) not showing; no discharge or watering. |
| **Faeces** | Should be firm, with no persistent constipation or diarrhoea. |
| **Movement** | Free movement, agile, with no stiffness in joints or gait; weight evenly distributed. |
| **Skin** | It should be supple, with no scurf, inflammation, parasites or sores. |
| **Teeth** | The teeth should be clean; gums should be pink, not inflamed or white or yellowish; no bad breath. |
| **Urine** | It should be passed effortlessly with no pain. |

# Vaccinations

There are many diseases to which kittens and cats are prone, but, fortunately, three of the most serious illnesses, Feline Infectious Enteritis, Feline Leukaemia Virus and feline upper respiratory disease (more commonly known as Feline Influenza or 'cat flu'), can be prevented by vaccination. It is strongly recommended that you have your kitten or cat vaccinated against all these potentially fatal diseases.

▲ Regular booster vaccinations will give your pet a lifelong protection from the major illnesses that are most likely to threaten it.

## Feline Infectious Enteritis

This is the most serious disease, and it spreads so quickly through a neighbourhood, leaving so many cats dead, that people often think that there has been widespread poisoning. Young cats are particularly vulnerable, and the disease is at its worst in summer. The symptoms are a sudden rise in the cat's temperature and the refusal of food. The cat sits huddled up, often near a water bowl or a sink, without taking any water. It vomits occasionally, cries faintly when it is picked up, and passes blood-stained motions. Death can occur within 24 hours.

## Feline Leukaemia Virus (FeLV)

Young kittens are more susceptible to FeLV and so it is more important to vaccinate them. The virus can cause suppression of their immune system or tumours and it is usually fatal.

## Feline Influenza

The symptoms of 'cat flu' are running of the eyes and nose, sneezing and, later, congestion of the lungs. The cat should be kept quiet and warm, and veterinary help should be obtained at once. Cats may die of this disease, so prompt attention and careful nursing are essential.

A blocked nose is another common symptom, along with a loss of appetite because the cat is unable to smell its food or because it has painful ulcers in its mouth. Once a cat has had cat flu, it will almost certainly carry the virus in the lining of its nose for the rest of its life.

## Vaccinations are vital

At around the age of 12 weeks, kittens may be vaccinated against Feline Infectious Enteritis, Feline Leukaemia Virus (FeLV) and 'cat flu'. Booster vaccinations should be given regularly. Your veterinary surgeon will advise you how often these are needed.

# Household dangers

▶ Kittens love exploring and you should take care not to leave any toxic substances lying around in the home or garden.

Many people keep their kittens confined to the kitchen as this room is usually warm and easily cleaned. However, the kitchen of a normal home is often full of potential danger to an inquisitive, mischievous little cat. Here are some general guidelines to how to make your home safer.

● **Paints, sprays and solvents**
Most of these are highly toxic to cats, not only when they are taken internally, but also if absorbed through the skin or the paw pads. The vapours, being heavier than air, sink to floor level, and so affect pets more than humans, giving rise to a severe toxic reaction.

▼ Many kittens will enjoy playing with wires or even live electric cables. Make sure no trailing wires are available.

● **Electrical cables** Kittens find trailing electrical cables very attractive, pouncing, grasping the flex in all four sets of claws and then biting it hard. If live, the wire can give the kitten a fatal shock. Even if switched off and unplugged, trailing flex may tempt a kitten to play, and its weight could cause a heavy iron or kettle to fall on to it.

● **Household cleaning products** Most of these are toxic to all felines.

● **Electrical appliances** A nervous new kitten may crawl into the back opening of the washing machine, tumble dryer, dishwasher or refrigerator, or, indeed, may crawl through any hole in the back of a kitchen cupboard and become trapped. Attracted to the warmth, kittens have been recorded as climbing inside washing machines and dryers and curling up to sleep. If unnoticed, the machine could be switched on with fatal results. Chimneys are also notoriously attractive to kittens.

◀ Windows that are left open can be dangerous for both kittens and cats, especially if they are house cats or the open window is on an upper storey of the house.

● **Hobs and hotplates** Kittens have been scalded with liquids from pans and kettles in the best managed of kitchens. Even when switched off, hotplates can burn delicate paw pads.

● **Thread and wool** A kitten will be fascinated by trailing sewing thread or wool. Once it starts to swallow a length of thread it is unable to pull it back out of the throat. It will keep swallowing until the needle is wedged in the mouth or swallowed, when emergency veterinary treatment is needed.

● **House plants** Kittens are naturally attracted to the dangling leaves of house plants. Many species are poisonous, so keep well out of reach.

◀ Many plants in the garden as well as inside the house are poisonous and you should ensure that your kitten does not come into contact with them. Beware of sweet peas, rhododendrons, azaleas, clematis and flowering laburnum.

# Ailments

## Abscesses

With a longhaired kitten, daily combing will quickly show up any abscess, swelling or wound which may be hidden in the long fur and for which veterinary treatment might be needed. With a shorthaired kitten, daily observation and handling should reveal any wounds that might need expert handling.

## Allergies

Allergies are fairly common in kittens and have a variety of causes. Some kittens are allergic to milk and dairy products (see page 22) while, in others, fish may cause a dry and irritating skin condition along the base of the spine. Parasites, such as fleas, can initiate a similar irritating eczema, particularly in the warm summer months. Houseplants, household cleaning products, sprays and some man-made fibres may be responsible for making your pet ill. Any persistent diarrhoea, vomiting or discarge of the eyes could point to an allergy, and a complete veterinary check is advisable.

▼ Kittens that groom themselves can swallow lots of loose hairs that matt up in the stomach and form hair balls. You should groom your kitten regularly to prevent this.

## Digestive complaints and hair balls

In slight cases of these complaints, the kitten will provide its own remedy by eating grass. It is therefore very important for town kittens or cats to have access to grass, even if it is only in a window box or specially grown in a flowerpot. Occasional constipation can be relieved by a tablespoonful of medicinal paraffin or olive oil (half a tablespoonful for a kitten under six months), which can be repeated twice daily for two days. For any more serious digestive upset, like persistent vomiting, veterinary advice should be sought at once.

## Ear problems

There are different causes for what is often referred to as 'canker' of the ear; only your vet can make a diagnosis and give the appropriate treatment. There may be a foreign body (a grass seed, for example) in the ear, although a common cause of ear trouble is the presence of a mite which lives and breeds in the wax deep down in the ear. If your kitten or cat shakes its head in pain and scratches its ear, you should seek veterinary help straight away as the ear is extremely delicate.

## Eyes

If you suspect that your kitten might have an eye problem, take it to your veterinary surgeon immediately. The first signs will often be a weeping eye, or one that is swollen or partly closed. Sick kittens will sometimes show the third eyelid which looks like a film across the eye.

## Serious illnesses

The most serious common illnesses that are likely to afflict cats and kittens are Feline Infectious Enteritis, Feline Influenza ('cat flu') and Feline Leukaemia (FeLV) . These diseases can be guarded against effectively through a programme of immunization (see page 35).

## Skin diseases

If sore or bald patches or pimples appear on a kitten's skin, veterinary help is needed. It is dangerous to apply medication, e.g. ointment, without veterinary advice, since the kitten may well be poisoned by licking it off. Besides, there are many different causes of similar-looking conditions. There may be mange or ringworm, which are serious if neglected but easily cured by the right treatment. Skin problems can also be caused by fleas or lice, or may be due to some internal complaint, such as kidney disease, which obviously needs veterinary treatment.

## Teeth

The teeth should be checked regularly for build-up of tartar, which can lead to gum disease (gingivitis) and the premature loss of teeth. If you suspect a problem, then seek veterinary advice.

## Vomiting

Vomiting in kittens may be serious, especially if the substance brought up resembles frothy, beaten egg whites, or is a bright yellow liquid. Vomiting which is accompanied by diarrhoea and a high temperature is a warning of some serious disease and the kitten will need urgent veterinary attention. If the kitten regurgitates undigested food you have no cause for alarm; it has merely eaten too much, or too quickly.

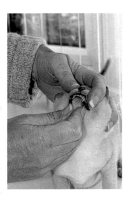

▲ Inspect the kitten's mouth: the gums should be pink and the teeth should be clean.

# Parasites

▶ Fleas are disagreeable for both the kitten and its owner. Your veterinary surgeon can advise on the best treatment. You can use a flea comb to remove fleas but it is not as effective as modern anti-flea medications.

## Fleas

Fleas can be found on even the best-kept kittens or cats. If you find some, ask your vet for an appropriate anti-flea remedy. This may be a spray or a spot-on product. It is important not to use an aerosol on a young kitten without first consulting your veterinary surgeon. Remember to deflea bedding, carpets, and corners as well. It's no use treating the kitten or

cat unless you thoroughly clean all the bedding and places where the kitten sleeps. Vacuuming the places where fleas can breed is every bit as important as treating the animal itself. If you think that vacuuming has not solved the problem, ask your veterinary surgeon for a surface anti-flea spray, to be used only on floors and never on the kitten.

▶ Most kittens and young cats are healthy and resilient. Good diet, exercise and careful observation will help keep them that way. If your kitten scratches and licks itself excessively, check that it has not got a parasite infestation.

## Worms

Both kittens and cats can become infected with two sorts of worms: roundworms and tapeworms. The roundworm is round in cross-section and measures 5–15 cm (2–6 in) long. It can be a particular problem in kittens (which often pick up the worms from their mother), so they should be treated against roundworms at the age of four weeks and then repeatedly until they are six months old.

Tapeworms are inclined to affect older animals and are caught from an intermediate host which, depending on the species of tapeworm, may be either a flea or a small rodent. If you suspect your kitten has worms, ask your veterinary surgeon for the correct treatment. Treat adults for both sorts of worms every three months throughout adult life.

## Life cycle of the tapeworm

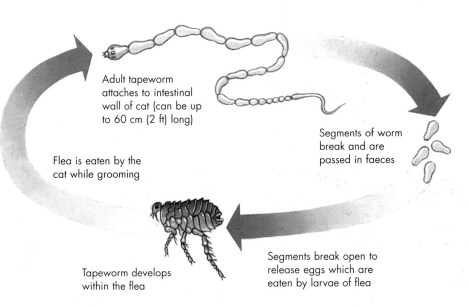

Adult tapeworm attaches to intestinal wall of cat (can be up to 60 cm (2 ft) long)

Segments of worm break and are passed in faeces

Flea is eaten by the cat while grooming

Tapeworm develops within the flea

Segments break open to release eggs which are eaten by larvae of flea

## Lice

Cats may also be affected by lice which are more difficult to see than fleas, although their white eggs, or nits, show up well, particularly on dark fur. Cats that constantly lick and bite themselves may be infested with lice, and should be taken to a veterinary surgeon for examination. The veterinary surgeon will be able to prescribe a good spray that will need to be used for at least a month.

# Giving medicine

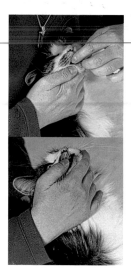

Kittens can sometimes be difficult patients when it comes to taking their medicine. However, once you know the basic guidelines to follow, administering medication can be much easier for both patient and owner.

● **Tablets** First, hold your kitten or cat securely on a non-slip surface. It is probably easiest if two people are on hand: one to administer the tablet, and the other to hold the cat's front legs, gently but firmly, from behind. Alternatively, wrap the kitten or cat securely in a blanket.

Put your left hand (if you are right-handed) on the top of the kitten's head, press your thumb and forefinger against the side of its jaws, and gently tilt the head back. The mouth should now be slightly open. With your right hand (which should be clean with fairly short fingernails), quickly put the tablet as far back down the kitten's throat as possible. Close up the mouth and gently stroke the back of the throat to help the pill move down the gullet. A very large tablet can always be broken up into smaller pieces.

▲ To give a tablet, hold the head back and ease the tablet in to the mouth. Gently rub the throat until the cat swallows.

● **Liquid medicine** Follow the procedure above and gently pull out the cheek to form a pouch into which medicine can be trickled from a spoon, or small plastic syringe, a few drops at a time. Be sure to give the kitten enough time to swallow.

● **Ear drops** Hold the kitten's head to one side and insert the drops using the applicator supplied. Gently massage behind the ear to help the drops penetrate. Clean away any surplus drops from the ear with great care.

● **Eye drops** Hold the kitten's head back and apply the eye drops to the inner corner of the eye using the applicator supplied. Keep the head back for a while to allow the drops to cover the whole surface of the eye.

◄ Give medicines by holding back the head and spooning them into the cat's mouth.

# First aid

In an emergency, do not rush to the veterinary surgery without checking that someone will be there. Phone first. There are several things you can do while waiting for professional help.

- First, make sure that the kitten is breathing without obstruction. This might necessitate clearing the airway by pulling the tongue forward – hold it with a handkerchief and take care not to get bitten.
- Staunch any major bleeding by placing a clean, folded handkerchief over the wound and then pressing firmly enough to stop the blood flow.
- Shock can be countered by keeping the kitten as quiet as possible, preferably in a darkened room, and as warm as possible by covering with a blanket, applying a well-wrapped hot water bottle or raising the temperature of the room overall.
- To apply artificial respiration, ideally the kitten should be on its right side, with the head and neck extended and the tongue pulled forward. Place your hand over the ribs just behind the shoulder blade, compress the chest cavity, then relax the pressure, allowing the chest to expand naturally. Repeat at five- to six-second intervals.
- Take great care in moving an injured kitten. If it seems that it has sustained a fracture, avoid moving it at all if possible. Never try to apply a splint or bandage. Wait calmly for help to arrive. If, after a car accident, a kitten must be moved straight away, slide it carefully on to a tray and use as a stretcher. If no fracture is suspected, use a secure carrier to transport the cat to the vet. A strong grocery box is suitable if the sides are pierced for ventilation and the top tied down.

▲ In an emergency, keep the cat warm and quiet and be careful and gentle if you have to move it. Place a hot water bottle, covered with a cloth, next to the cat.

▼ Check the breathing, opening the mouth and pulling the tongue forwards. You can give heart massage by rubbing the area over the heart with both hands; don't use too much force.

# Your questions answered

### I think my kitten has worms, but how can I tell?

Many kittens have roundworm from birth and in the early stages do not show many symptoms except perhaps a pot belly. Sometimes the worms, looking like pieces of very thin white string, are seen in the faeces. It is important not to let a kitten go untreated as a heavy infestation will interfere with digestion, and the kitten will not thrive as it should. Consequently, 'worming' should be routine and your veterinary surgeon will advise on a suitable dosage. Another type of worm that is found in a cat's digestive system is the tapeworm, and its presence can often be detected by segments of the worm, which resemble grains of rice and are seen around the anus. Medicine for roundworm will not kill a tapeworm, and treatment should be given under veterinary supervision.

### When playing in the garden, our four-month-old kitten often dashes under the car parked in the drive and emerges with streaks of oil along its back. How can it be removed safely?

Oil must be removed from the kitten's coat without delay as it is highly toxic if it is absorbed through the coat or tongue. Any lumps or thick patches should be carefully wiped from the coat with toilet tissue, then the residue washed off with a mild household detergent. Once the oil has been removed, rinse all traces of detergent from the coat and dry the kitten thoroughly. If the kitten is heavily coated in oil, waste no time in taking it to your veterinary surgeon. Wipe away as much of the substance as possible, and make sure that the kitten does not lick its coat by wrapping its body in a towel.

Kittens should be kept away from oil, grease and wet paint. Garages are dangerous places for young kittens as there are not only sharp tools but also the possibility of the kitten licking anti-freeze which could prove lethal. Kittens are also likely to crawl up into the engine of a vehicle, or on to a tyre and out of sight. If the vehicle is started before the kitten is discovered, it could result in tragedy.

**I know that my kitten must be expected to claw the furniture, but is there anything I can do to discourage it, or will it just grow out of it?**

Cats will always need to sharpen their claws, and they will not be able to differentiate 'naturally' between an oak tree and an antique sideboard! However, they can and should be trained from kittenhood not to claw certain things. You should provide a suitable scratching post (see page 31), and each time your kitten attempts to scratch the furniture, clap your hands together and say 'No' sharply. Then encourage the kitten to use the scratching post instead by placing its forepaws on the surface and making slight scratching movements with them. With patience, the kitten should soon learn.

**I worry when my little kitten gets stuck up a tree. What is the best way to get it down?**

Climbing as high as possible seems to be a favourite activity with cats; many will happily spend the day on the ridge of a roof or stretched out on a lofty branch. Just because your kitten does not come down does not mean that it can't – but the kitten may be intimidated by a sea of upturned, calling faces down below.

Even if it is mewing and would obviously like to come down, it is probably best to let it work out its own plan of descent. With its highly developed sense of balance, the kitten is unlikely to fall. You may leave it there safely for several hours and, if left alone, perhaps with a plate of strong-smelling food at the base of the tree, curiosity or hunger (or greed!) will usually be sufficient enticement. If you do decide to climb up the tree, take a zip-up bag or strong pillow case into which you can pop the kitten before bringing it down.

**As my kitten is infested with fleas, we have bought some flea powder. But will it be dangerous if it licks its fur after the powder has been applied – would a spray have been safer?**

A veterinary-recommended product is generally more effective than a powder, but either must be applied exactly in accordance with the manufacturer's instructions, taking great care to avoid the kitten's eyes and genital region. After application, keep the kitten amused while the product does its work, then brush and comb the coat to remove dead fleas, debris and the residue of the insecticide.

# Life history

| | |
|---|---|
| **Scientific name** | *Felis catus* |
| **Gestation period** | 63 days (approx.) |
| **Litter size** | 3–5 (average) |
| **Birth weight** | 90 g (3 oz) – 140 g (5 oz) |
| **Eyes open** | 10 days |
| **Weaning age** | 42–56 days |
| **Puberty** | 120–180 days |
| **Adult weight** | Males: 3.5 kg (8 lb) – 5.9 kg (13 lb)<br>Females: 2.25 kg (5 lb) – 3 kg (7 lb) |
| **Best age to breed** | 12+ months |
| **Oestrus (or season)** | Repeatedly in season January–October unless mated |
| **Duration of oestrus** | 7–14 days |
| **Retire from breeding** | Males: 10 years<br>Females: 8 years |
| **Life expectancy** | 12–16 years |

# Index

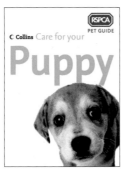

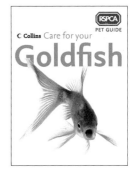